Adobe Ph

A Beginners Guide to Adobe Photoshop

Preface

Adobe Photoshop has become one of the best tools available today when it comes to editing photos and designing websites. Although there may be a lot of tools involved in the software, it is also one of those that give the best output when it comes to designing.

To help you start learning this powerful program, start with the basics of Adobe Photoshop to learn and master the tools and to avoid any frustrations in your work, Indeed, a little patience in learning the tools and the basics can help keep your enthusiasm and interest in learning and using the program in your projects. Here are some basic tools that you may want to familiarize to start with Adobe Photoshop.

Understanding the Interface

Of course, before you start, you have to understand the workspace where you will be working on in Photoshop. In the Adobe Photoshop workspace, you will see your toolbox found on the left side of your workspace. This contains the tools that you will be using for your editing and designing, although you can still find a lot of tools in the menu bar and the options bar, which is located right below the menu bar, which you may be familiar with already.

These tools may be represented with icons of pencils, small arrows, medicine dropper and many others which will help you take note of their function.

On the right side of your workspace, you will find other palettes that will provide you with options and important information about the document you have in your workspaces such as its colors as well as the changes that you have done with the image or document.

Understanding the Tools

If it is your first time with the program, you may be overwhelmed by the many icons in its toolbox and you may be overwhelmed with what to use when. For beginners, it is important to understand the basics. You may want to group these tools according to their function to make them easier to keep in mind.

The Adobe Photoshop tools include tools that allow you to select such as the Marquee, the Lasso, and the Magic Wand. You can find them at the top of the toolbox which is represented by a dotted square, an irregularly shaped polygon and a magic wand respectively and these are used depending on the size or the shape of the object or image that you want to select in your document.

You will also find the brush, which is one of the basic tools that you will be using, the eraser, the blur or the sharpen tool and most especially the clone stamp. The clone stamp has been one of the many important tools in Photoshop that you will find amazing, as it will copy a particular image in the picture, and useful if you want to create more trees, or delete someone in the background.

You can also make use of the drawing tools as well as the tools that allow you to copy existing colors in your image. Mastering these two is the very basics of Adobe Photoshop, thus before getting too excited to start with your project, learn these tools and master their function.

Thank you for choosing to read this book. Read on and I'm sure it will be instrumental in building your Photoshop skills.

Table of Content

Bonus: preview of: Google Drive: A Beginner's Guide to Google Drive: Master Google Drive, Docs, Sheets, and Slides Now 131

Chapter 1

Getting Started with Photoshop

What is Photoshop?

Photoshop is the industry standard tool for image editing, and with good reason. It is flexible, powerful and has evolved over many years to include all of the features that you need to edit images for both print and the web. Photoshop is easily extensible, with a huge number of filters, effects and plugins available to help to speed up common tasks.

Downloading Photoshop

Adobe Photoshop has the easiest ways to maneuver and also has helpful elements; the beginning designers can easily capture the process, procedure, elements, editing picture and overall everything for this. Also possible to do clipping paths, image masking, raster to vector, image manipulation, image retouching, Photoshop layer masking, photo restoration, and high end retouching all kinds of design-related job which are much helpful in the design sector.

With adobe Photoshop software there has a lot of software as like adobe illustrator (we can make each thing individually), paint.net (possible to edit photo by this), CorelDRAW Graphics Suite, GIMP (open source software and free bitmap image editor as like adobe Photoshop), Inkscape (this is also open source software and is a free vector image editor which is similar to Adobe Illustrator), Scribus (this is a free desktop publishing tool similar to Adobe QuarkxPress or InDesign), FontForge (is a free font creator and editor), did (this is also a free tool for creating diagrams), gPick (is a free color scheme generator), pixie, seashore, Xara Xtreme, choco flop, PhotoPlus, CinePaint, mac preview, PhotoFiltre also there are plenty helpful software and tools for creating creative design.

But all time that's not possible to buy the software, so we always feel the necessity download its free version. With old to update all versions we have found on the internet. But generally we always think those update versions are worthwhile for us because of its helpful updated tools. But before downloading the software we need free space, also should fix that it's for Windows 7 (32 bit), Windows 7 (64 bit), Windows Vista (32 bit), Windows Vista (64 bit), Windows XP or it's for mac.

For download software we normally search that free download of software adobe Photoshop or something like that. Then we can see some of the add as like download via cNet, freeware or filehippo.com etc. After that we will go with one site and will download our expected software and by downloading free software we will enjoy by use.

Features of Photoshop

Among various features of Photoshop the following ten features are most important and mostly used.

1. Alternate ways to open files
2. Layers and Groups
3. Document navigation
4. Creating New Files
5. Cropping
6. Resetting Photoshop's preferences and Plugin Folder when Launching
7. Layer Styles
8. Preset manager and Tool presets
9. ACR
10. Printing and Soft Proofing

How to install Photoshop

The following steps will show you how to install Photoshop on your computer.

1. Browse for the setup.exe in your DVD/ Downloaded.

2. Run Setup.exe.

3. Wait for setup to start, a dialog box will open.

4. Read the agreement and click install.

5. Enter your license number or click to install as trial, select your Language and continue

6. Create your adobe ID or skip

7. Choose directory to install your product

8. Click on button Install, this screen will appear. Wait for some time and you are finished.

9. You are done! Now you can begin.

Chapter 2

Knowing the Work Area

Customizing your Workspace

Mastering the Interface

Before you can get started with Photoshop, the first thing that you should do is learn your way around the software. The Photoshop interface can be confusing at first, but it is very flexible and you can configure it to suit your needs. You can break the interface up into panels, and show only the panels that you need. You can even pre-define different layouts for different tasks and switch between them at will.

Managing Panels

Panels are the elements that make up the broader Photoshop interface. Most of the work that you do inside Photoshop will involve panels. There are panels for layers, adjustments, colors and textures, channels and even your edit history. The sheer number of channels available might be overwhelming at first. That's why it's a good idea to learn your way around the user interface and familiarize yourself with each feature before you start working through more complex tutorials. It may not seem like the most exciting thing to do, but it will make life a lot easier in the long run.

Before you begin, let's make sure that you are starting from the default settings.

If you have experimented with Photoshop before you might have made some changes to the panels and the layout, and this can make following tutorials a little confusing. The working environment in Photoshop is called a workspace. The default workspace is a good starting point for inexperienced users. You can add or remove panels and reposition them, then save the workspace so that Photoshop knows how it should have the panels laid out the next time you run it.

Make sure that you are running the default workspace by looking at the top right-hand corner of the Photoshop user interface, just below the minimize, maximize and close buttons. There is a workspace selection box there. This box is not labeled so it is easy to overlook. If you are using the default layout the box should say Essentials. If it says anything else, then change the drop-down to say Essentials so that you are using a standard layout.

If may take a few seconds for the interface to update depending on the performance of your computer. You may see some panels open or close, and some move around. To confirm that you are really using the default layout, click on the word Essentials inside the selection box and then select Reset Essentials from the menu that appears. You are now using the default layout for Photoshop.

In the default layout, there are two-panel columns. The right-hand side of the screen features the main column and there is a secondary, narrower column to the left of it. Photoshop has three panels in the main column. These panels show the tools that are the most frequently used by the average user.

The top panel is the Color panel, which allows you to select the color of your text, brushes, fills and other tools. Below that is the Adjustments panel, which shows tools for adjusting brightness, gamma, hue, saturation and other image properties. Below that is the Layers panel, which is used to merge, move and edit layers. Each panel is clearly labeled; their name appears in a tab at the top of the panel.

Panel Groups

While there are only three panels visible, the main column contains more than just those three panels. There are other panels in the column, in "panel groups". For example, in a tab adjacent to the Color panel tab there is the Swatches panel tab. Selecting tabs is simple, just click on the tab name. This is something that you should be familiar with doing from other software applications. In fact, using most features of Photoshop is pretty easy.

The difficulty for newest users is under- standing what a feature is called and where it can be located in the menu. The Swatches tab is a tab that allows you to select from a pre-defined selection of colors. This is good if you are working with images that can only have a limited number of colors in them due to printing restrictions. When you click on a tab, the other tabs in that group move to the background.

The existing configuration of panels and groups in the Essentials workspace is a good starting point for most users, but if you don't like them for some reason you can re-order them. For example, you may find that you use the Styles panel more often than the

Adjustments panel. In this case you can move the Styles panel to the front of the panel group so that it is the first one you see. To do this, simply click on the tab that you want to move and hold the mouse button down while you drag the tab to the position that you want it, then release the mouse button. Panel Groups

While there are only three panels visible, the main column contains more than just those three panels. There are other panels in the column, in "panel groups". For example, in a tab adjacent to the Color panel tab there is the Swatches panel tab. Selecting tabs is simple, just click on the tab name. This is something that you should be familiar with doing from other software applications. In fact, using most features of Photoshop is pretty easy. The difficulty for newest users is understanding what a feature is called and where it can be located in the menu.

The Swatches tab is a tab that allows you to select from a pre-defined selection of colors. This is good if you are working with images that can only have a limited number of colors in them due to printing restrictions. When you click on a tab, the other tabs in that group move to the background.

The existing configuration of panels and groups in the Essentials workspace is a good starting point for most users, but if you don't like them for some reason you can re-order them. For example, you may find that you use the Styles panel more often than the Adjustments panel. In this case you can move the Styles panel to the front of the panel group so that it is the first one you see. To do this, simply click on the tab that you want to move and hold the mouse button down while you drag the tab to the position that you want it, then release the mouse button.

Palettes in Photoshop

Think of the History palette as Photoshop's very own time machine. It holds a list of your most recent steps, and lets you undo the changes you made with those steps by reverting your image to a previous state. The number of steps which are held in memory can be specified through Edit -> Preferences -> Performance or, for Mac users, Photoshop -> Preferences -> Performance, and modifying the value in the History States box.

The History palette has some handy shortcuts for fast access, just like most of the other tools

Since there are a limited number of past states available to you, you might want to create a document 'snapshot' at certain stages of design as a manual backup that you can go back to if things go wrong later on. This can be done by clicking on the tiny triangle present on the right corner of the History palette and choosing New Snapshot. A snapshot of the current layer, the entire document or merged layers can be made depending on your choice.

Photoshop's default workspace setup has the following:

- Menu bar: You'll most likely already have seen menu bars in other programs on your computer. Menu bar will run across your Photoshop window's top, and will contain different options for the software's tools.

- Toolbox: The toolbox will be present on the left side of the Photoshop window, it will be the place from where you select Photoshop's various tools.

- Options bar: This bar will be present under menu bar and will contain contextualized options for various tools i.e. depending on the tool you have a selection; it will hold different options. It will also hold the workspace menu from where you can load and save palette arrangements.

Like professionals belonging to most other specialist fields, designers have their own dictionary of terms. A comp (an abbreviation for 'composite'), for instance, is a rough draft of the final solution planned by the designer 'Comp' traditionally refers to page layouts in the print world, but web designers normally use it to refer to an unchanging interface made completely in Photoshop that their clients can assess and then decide whether to proceed with the site development or not. You may even come across the word being used as a verb: 'comping' refers to the process of making a mockup site.

Palettes:

These are individual panes which hold options or information for working with your file. They float on the right-hand side the window and each of them is labeled with a tab. One can close palettes, minimize palettes, group palettes with others, or drag palettes in / out of a panel dock at will.

Document windows: Each document that you open in Photoshop will have its own window, with a status bar along its bottom. The status bar is present to the right side of the zoom percentage shown in the bottom left corner, and displaces information that is specific to the opened document.

Personalizing the workspace

You can change your Photoshop's workspace to suit the project you're working on – or even to your particular tastes for every project.

Nearly everything inside the workspace can be reconfigured and repositioned. Here are some ways to do this:

Changing menu bar's look:

You can modify the menu items that are visible on your menu bar, and can even add colors to these items. If you wish, you can also assign different or totally new keyboard shortcuts to menu comments (not recommended until you're very much at home with Photoshop or have an urgent reason to do so). Navigate to Edit on the Menus, then use the dialog box to change menu bar / palette menus.

Options bar:

If you wish to move this bar around, click where the handle is on its left side and drag around with your mouse. The options bar can 'dock' onto the bottom or top of the screen when you move it close to those areas.

Moving the toolbox:

The Photoshop toolbox is very portable and you can move it to any part of your screen. Click on notched handle on its top and drag it around. You can also switch between various toolbox layouts by clicking on the double arrow along the toolbox's top.

Rearranging palettes:

There are plenty of ways for rearranging the palettes. You may wish to separate one palette from its palette group or move it to another group entirely. This can be through dragging on the palette's tab outside of its original group and into the new one. You may also wish to collapse or expand a dock

- do this by clicking the double arrows at its top. You can also drag some palettes out of their dock and then close the remaining ones. If you accidentally close a palette and want to open it again go to the Window menu and click on the palette you wish to show.

Changing the information being shown on the document window's status bar:

The status bar will display the size of the document by default. This file size is shown by two numbers that are separated by a forward slash. The first number estimates the size of the image file with all of the layers (more on these to come) merged together (this is known as flattening the image), while the second number estimates the size of the document with all the layers as they are. Don't be confused by the technicality of the previous sentence, since layers will be discussed in detail in the next chapter. You can make the status bar display information other than the file size though e.g. the dimensions of the document in pixels, or the version of the file. This can be done by clicking on the arrow present next to the status bar and choosing the information you want to see.

Saving the customized workspace:

As one becomes skilled at using Photoshop, you will find yourself using certain palette sets for different kinds of projects quite frequently, and then there may be those palettes that you rarely or never use. Photoshop lets you save or even load various workspaces (these are unique arrangements of palettes, menus and even keyboard shortcuts) to make your work more efficient.

Once you have customized your workspace as needed, open the Workspace menu in the options bar, click on Save Workspace and give your workspace a name e.g. My Default Workspace or Creating Thumbnails. You can then load various saved (or already present) workspaces by opening the Workspace menu and selecting the workspace from it.

Chapter 3

Working in Photoshop

Creating New Documents

The first thing to do after you open the application is either create a new document or open existing documents. In order to create a new document you can choose File> New or use shortcut by pressing Ctrl + N (Windows) or Command + N (MAC).

New document dialog box will appear. You can directly name the file by filling up the name column or just leave it untitled and do it later when you save the file.

Go under the File menu and choose New to bring up the New dialog. This is where you choose the size and resolution of your new document—just type in the Width and Height you want, along with the Resolution (in this case, I choose 240 Pixels/ Inch for printing to an inkjet printer). You can also choose the color you want for your background (in case you don't want it to be white), and a color profile, if you like. At the top of the dialog is the Document Type pop-up menu, which contains presets with common image sizes and resolutions already in place—you can choose web presets, print presets, video presets, and so on. If you have a particular custom size you use (like maybe for printing on 13x19" paper), you can save that as your own custom preset. Just enter the size and resolution you want (again, I use 240 ppi for inkjet printing), and click the Save Preset button at the top right. Name your preset and now it will appear in the Document Type pop-up menu for next time.

Preset allows you to choose and use some fixed sizes of standard papers, such as U.S. Paper (Letter, Legal, Tabloid), International Paper (A4, A5, A6, etc.), Photo (2x3, 4x6, etc.), and many more.

Next, you can fill up the width and height of your document, by default they will be in pixels (standard measuring size for web usage). You may change them according to your needs by clicking on those columns.

For resolution, leave it at 72 pixels/ inch for web or standard usage, while for printing purposes you should enter 300 pixels/ inch.

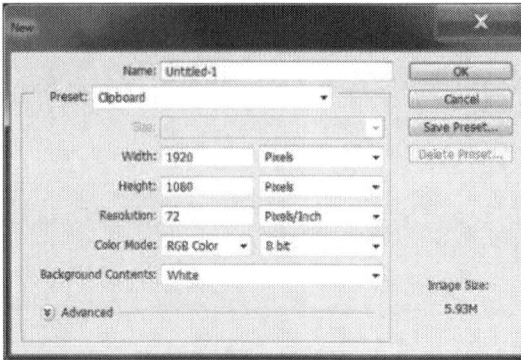

Select RGB as color mode for standard usage, while for printing you need to choose CMYK as the color mode.

The background contents is the background color you start with your document, you can choose white or transparent background to start with. After filling them all, click the OK button or press Enter.

New workspace will show up, this is where you put all your work. Note that you can also create more documents as much as needed and there will be new tabs created for each document

You can create a new document in Photoshop by opening File > New from the menu, or by using the Ctrl+N keys / Command+N keys from your keyboard, depending on whether you're using a PC or a Mac. The New dialog box will show up you can specify the dimensions, as well as many other settings for your documents here.

Opening Files:

You can open an existing file by File > Open from the menu, or by using the Ctrl+O/Command+O keyboard combinations. You can also select multiple files to open by holding down the Ctrl/Command button on your keyboard and clicking on each file you wish to open.

Saving Files:

You can save your work to File > Save, or by pressing Ctrl+S/Command+S from the keyboard. Photoshop saves in the PSD (Photoshop Document) format by default, but you can choose any format you wish from the list in the Save dialog box. Note that if you're working with layers, it is recommended that you save your document in PSD format to preserve them – saving in a standard format such as JPEG will cause Photoshop to merge all layers together to create a final document, meaning that you won't be able to change the individual layers anymore.

You can also save a copy of your work using the Ctrl+Shift+S keys or the File > Save As option from the menu. A pro tip is to save your original document as PSD (so you can modify it later), and then save copies as standard formats such as JPEG, BMP etc.

Snappy Presets:

If you're working on a picture with a size of, say, 1024 x 768 pixels, then you should start with a smaller size of 800 x 600. Notice how the ratio of horizontal pixels to vertical pixels remains the same? This is extremely important if you're going to be playing with multiple resolutions. Also make sure that you set the correct resolution – expressed in dots-per-inches – so your final image doesn't look ugly once it gets blown up to actual size. As a newbie in Photoshop, I once accidentally saved a masterfully edited photograph at a resolution smaller than its original one – and although it looked good on my laptop's screen, the results were far from pretty when I printed it on A5 sized (large) paper.

Saving files for the internet:

Photoshop files (i.e. PSDs) cannot directly be placed on the internet or even in a Word document for that matter. They need to be exported to an internet friendly format such as PNG, JPEG or GIF. These formats also normally take up less space than bitmaps (BMPs).

- GIF: Pronounced as 'gift' or 'jiff' depending on your personal preference, this format supports a maximum of 256 different colors. This format also has support for transparency and animation (ever seen those small moving clips people often share in Facebook comments?), and is ideal for graphics that have the large areas of exactly the same color e.g. company logos, watermarks etc.

- JPEG: Pronounced as 'jay-peg', this format is best for photographs or graphics which have greater than 256 colors and gradients (gradual change from one color to another), for instance a landscape picture or a close up portrait. JPEG format will compress the image so it won't have a result as good as the uncompressed bitmap image (BMP), but the compression will reduce its size, making it easier to store online and elsewhere.

- PNG: Portable Network Graphic, pronounced as 'ping' is the GIF format in the sense that it has support for transparency and is great for solid color pictures such as logos and icons. But it is also better than the GIF format thanks to supporting for true transparency levels for colored portions – this means that you can make a part of the picture partially see-through. PNGs can produce better-looking graphics while taking up lesser space than GIFs.

Photoshop lets you save your picture as a PNG-8 file (works just like a GIF) or a PNG-24 file (lets you save images with millions of colors as well as changing transparency levels).

The power of mouse clicks:

Besides the many keyboard shortcuts at your disposal, you can also use mouse clicks to do various tasks such as fitting the picture to the window, temporarily zoom in on the picture etc. These shortcut combinations are too many to be listed here, but you can always refer to Adobe's official list here http://bit.ly/default-keyboard-shortcuts if you're looking for a particular shortcut.

In order to save the file for Web, go to File > Save for Web & Devices or use the Ctrl+Alt+Shift+S keyboard combo (Command instead of Ctrl for Mac). The Save for Web dialog box will show up, where you will be able to see a preview of the image that you're about to export, with the optimized size in the lower left corner. You can play with the image settings using the many options present to the right.

Choose the format from GIF, PNG-8 and PNG-24, or JPEG, and change some of the other settings while observing the optimized file size value. You will need to strike a balance between file size and quality of the image. Once you're happy with the result, click on Save and give the picture a name.

After having tried out the exercise described above, you'll be quite happy with yourself about having saved an image of decent quality in a smaller size than the original. You did this by messing around with the settings on the right panel, but now it's time to learn what exactly they do:

GIF/PNG-8

Colors: Changing this setting lowers a number of colors present in the image. This will have a large impact on the final result of the picture.

Dither amount and type (Noise, Pattern, Diffusion, No Dither): This setting may seem scary, but there's really no need to get alarmed. Dither is the name given to a compression method which varies the pattern of dots to make the image seem to have a color gradient. Changing the dither setting will have a more visible impact on pictures which have lots of different colors mixed together.

Transparency: If you wish your image to have transparent areas, keep this box checked. Transparency will be looked at more closely in the next sections.

Matte color: For images which are transparent, matte color aids in blending the image's edges into the background of the document/page where it will be placed. Non-transparent images use matte color to define the color of their background. The use of matte color with transparent images will be looked at.

Chapter 4

User Interface in Photoshop

Photoshop Workspace

The Panels

Many of Photoshop's features are found within the
panels (they're kind of like palsites that pop out from
the side of the screen), and the most-often-used
panels are already visible onscreen by default (like
the Color panel, the Swatches panel, the Libraries
panel, the Layers panel, and so on) and appear on the
far right of the window. There's also a thin horizontal
panel across the top of the window called the Options
Bar (when you're using one of Photoshop's tools, it
shows all the options for that tool here).

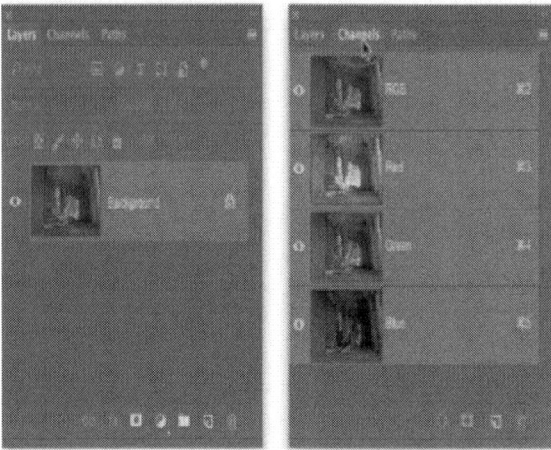

To keep your screen from being totally cluttered with panels, some panels are nested behind other panels, so all you see is a small tab sticking up with the name of the panel (see above left, where you see the Layers panel, and to the right of its tab you see two other tabs for panels that are nested with it the Channels panel and the Paths panel). To see one of these nested panels, just click on its tab, and the full panel appears (see above right, where I clicked on the Channels tab, and now you see the Channels panel). Of course, there are a lot more panels than what you see onscreen at first. To open any closed panel (there are around 30 in all), go to the Window menu (at the top of the screen), and you'll see all of them. Choose one and it opens onscreen, alongside the existing panels that are already open.

TIP: HOW TO MAKE PANELS "FLOAT"

If you want a particular panel to be detached from the rest, so it "floats" on its own, just click-and-drag a panel tab away from the rest of the panels and it "floats."

The Tools Panel Hiding and Closing the panel

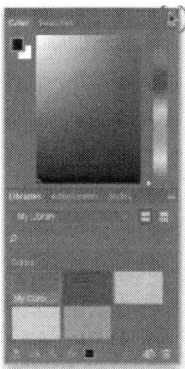

Open   Collapsed   Icons Only

47

You don't have to work with all your panels open all the time. You can collapse them down to just their icons and names, like you see above center (just click on the two little right-facing arrows in the top right of a panel, shown circled in red above left), or collapse them even further, so only their icons are showing (once you've collapsed them, click on the left edge of the panel group and drag to the right until just the icons are showing, as seen above right).

Collapsing these panels gives you a larger working area for your images, but your panels are still just one click away (click on any icon and that one panel pops out to full size). If you want to expand all the collapsed panels as a group (like you see above left), click on the two little left-facing arrows in the top right of the panel header. If you actually want to close a panel (not just collapse it; you want it off-screen altogether), click on the panel's tab and drag it away from the panels it's nested with (this makes it a floating panel), and now an "x" appears in the top-left corner of the panel.

Click on that to close it. To reopen it, go to the Window menu and choose it.

Seeing Multiple Images at once

When you open multiple images, they open kind of like panels do—you see the active image in front, and then little tabs (in the top of the image window) for the other open images behind it (if you have this tabbed viewing set in your Preferences). If you want to see all the images onscreen at the same time, go under the Window menu, under Arrange.

At the top of the menu are a bunch of choices for how you can display them: show them all in thin vertical tiles or horizontal tiles, or display two, three, four, or six images equally (like the four images I have onscreen here. When I choose 4-Up, it instantly resizes the image windows, so all four open images fit onscreen.

You'll see that I also have Application Frame turned on, here, in the Window menu [on a Mac]). If you look a little further down in the Arrange menu, you'll see some controls for making all those image windows open onscreen work together—what you do to an image window you click on, happens in all the other windows. For example, if you click on an image window and zoom in on that photo, then choose Match Zoom, the other three open images all zoom in the exact same way.

Organizing several Panels

When you choose to add a panel to what you see onscreen, in most cases, it just appears onscreen next to the ones you already have open. In many cases, they attach to the left edge of your already open panels, and they start to cover more and more of your image area. I personally prefer to keep all my panels in groups over on the right side of the window, so I have as much room for my images as possible.

If you like keeping things tidy like this, there are two things you can do:

1. You can group (nest) panels together by clicking on a panel's tab and dragging it onto another panel's tab. As you're dragging over onto the other panel you want to test it with, you'll see a blue stroke appear around the group of panels (as seen above left). Once you see that, just release your mouse button and it joins that group. So, you're pretty much dragging tabs together to form a group. Easy enough.

2. You can also attach panels directly below any open panel, pretty much the same way. But, in this case, you'll drag the tab to the bottom of a panel. When it's about to "dock," you'll see a solid blue line appear along the bottom of the panels you're about to dock with (as seen above

center). Now, just release the mouse button and it attaches to the bottom of the existing panels to form a vertical group

Use Guides

Anytime you need to line things up, you can drag out horizontal or vertical guides over your image. To get to these guides, first you have to make Photoshop's Rulers visible (press Command-R [PC: Ctrl-R]), then click-and-hold directly on the top or left-side ruler and drag out a guide, positioning it right where you want it. You can reposition them using the Move tool (V; when you move your cursor over a guide, it will change into a double-headed arrow with two lines in the middle. That's your cue that it's ready to move). If you want to add a guide based on a measurement (for example, you know you want a vertical guide added 2" into your image or 35 pixels into it, etc.), you can have Photoshop place it exactly at that position for you:

Go under the View menu and choose New Guide. In the dialog (seen in the inset above), enter the measurement you want (enter the number, then space, then "in" for inches, or "px" for pixels, etc.), click OK, and it places it precisely for you. To delete a guide, you don't want anymore, just drag it back to the ruler where it came from. To delete all your guides at once, go up under the View menu and choose Clear Guides.

Change the Color Outside My Image Area?

If you want to change the color of the workspace background outside your image, just Right-click anywhere outside your image (if you're using Application Frame with tabbed documents, you may need to shrink your image view a bit [zoom out]; if not, click-and-drag out your image window, so you can see the canvas area), and a pop-up menu will appear with choices. Choose the one you want and you're good to go.

Disable Pop-Up Tool Tips

Go under the Photoshop CC (PC: Edit) menu, under Preferences, and choose Tools. When the Preferences dialog opens, in the Options section, turn off the Show Tool Tips checkbox

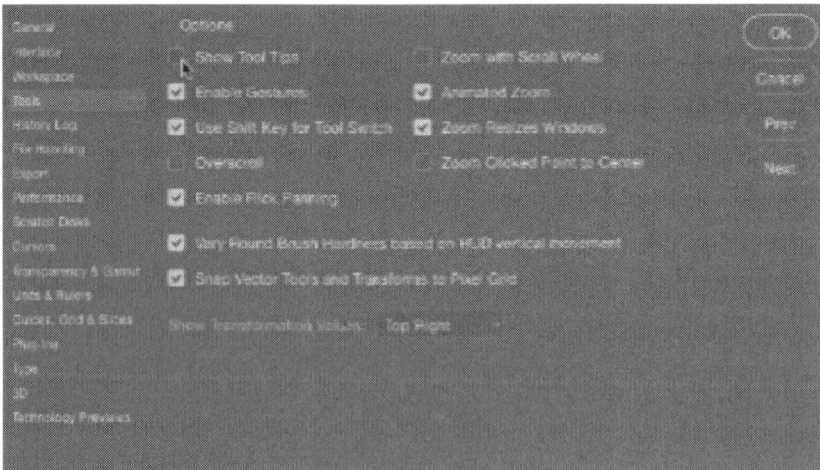

Change the Color of Photoshop's Interface?

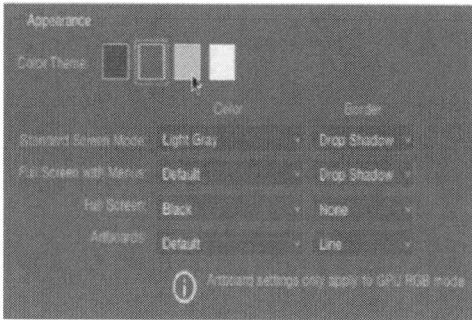

Go to the Photoshop CC (PC: Edit) menu, under Preferences, and choose Interface. When the Preferences dialog opens, in the Appearance section, choose a new interface color from the Color Theme color swatches. You don't really get to choose a new color here, you're just changing the lightness of the default gray color.

See My Image at Full-Screen Size?

Press the letter F on your keyboard twice. The first time you press it, it just hides the window that surrounds your image. But, the second time, it hides everything and displays your image full-screen size. Now, for some reason, one thing it doesn't hide in

Full-Screen mode is Photoshop's Rulers. So, if you have them visible, once you're in Full-Screen mode, press Command-R (PC: Ctrl-R) to hide them. To return to the regular size view (and see the rest of Photoshop), just press F again.

Make the Rulers Visible

Just press Command-R (PC: Ctrl-R) and rulers appear across the top and left side of your image window. That's it.

Change Starting Measurement

If, for some reason, you don't want the top-left corner of the image to be measured starting at the 0x0" point, you can click-and-hold directly in the top-left corner of the image window (not in the image, in the window—right where the vertical and horizontal rulers meet), and drag the starting point to a new location (for example, if you want to start measuring

2" into your image, you could drag the axis of those two rulers to that point and it starts measuring from there). Again, this is an advanced tip for you advanced folks who are advanced, and since you're advanced, all of that made sense. Hope that advances your advanced Photoshop skills.

Chapter 5

Photoshop Layers

One way to understanding Layers in Photoshop is to imagine you have thin transparent sheets of glass, these are our Layers. For this example, let's say three Layers. One of those Layers will be your background. The background Layer stays in place. All the Layers will be stacked on top of the background Layer allowing you to see through to the background image. So think of it as looking down through your stacks of transparent sheets of glass from the top sheet down through to your background sheet.

Your background Layer is an image of a rose. You can put a Layer with a picture of a hummingbird over the image of the rose, making it appear that the hummingbird is hovering over the rose. You may need to position your hummingbird to create the effect you want.

You might want to add raindrops, so you will take another Layer with the image of the raindrops and put it on top of the images of the hummingbird and the rose. In the stacking order in the Layers Panel each Layer will have the appearance of being stacked on top of each other but in the image window these stacks appear to be flattened, giving it the illusion of just the one picture.

Layers interact with each other through Opacity, (Opacity refers to the amount of transparency a Layer has). You can set the Opacity to complete transparency or opaque, meaning you can't see through it. By adjusting the Opacity settings you can have your background Layer partially show through the top Layer. The more you adjust the settings toward 0% Opacity, the top Layer becomes more transparent, allowing more of the background Layer to show through.

Now Let's say you want to change the color of the rose. You do all your edits to the rose on that one Layer, so you can make mistakes or even delete or replace it with another flower. Each edit is done on an individual Layer, which means you can go back and edit that particular Layer without the rest of your work being affected.

You can also change the stacking order in the Layers Panel. By changing the stacking order you can have the rain appear either behind or in front of the hummingbird.

You can turn each Layer on and off by clicking on the 'eye icon' next to the Layer you are working on. So if we wanted to see what the picture would look like without the rain, you just click on the 'eye icon' next to the Layer with the image of the rain on it turning that Layer off, making the Layer invisible.

The Layers are organized and displayed in the 'Layer's Panel' which is usually to the right of your image. You can also move the panel around. By keeping the panel visible you can tell which Layer you are working on just by glancing over and seeing which Layer is highlighted.

In my retouching tutorials I take the reader through the process of whitening the eyes, cleaning up blemishes with the Healing Brush, Airbrushing away those shiny patches and tidying the hair. If your new or relatively new to the concepts of Adobe Photoshop Elements 8, then this overview will help you understand the benefits of working with Layers throughout these processes.

At this stage I may decide that I am happy with my finished product. I now have the ability to flatten all the Layers into one, leaving me with all the finished edits which were on individual Layers, on the one Layer.

What are Layer Styles?

Layers were first introduced into Photoshop in 1994. Since then many other software programs have incorporated layers into their software. Layers can be considered the building blocks of digital images, and they help make your art more organized and easy to work with. You can create different versions of the same art with subtle differences all contained in one file. In this book we will look at all the aspects of layers in Adobe Photoshop Elements, including the layer panel, creating new layers, deleting layers, layer masks, adjustment layers, layer opacity, layer blending modes and more. Included are over one hundred screen shots to illustrate the concepts and techniques explained in the book.

The five most important characteristics of layers are as follows:

1. Opacity. Values lie between 0% (transparent) and 100% (completely opaque).

2. Holes, in pixel layers, either where you have erased or deleted image data or where they are smaller than the layer beneath and allow underlying details to show through. This is particularly useful for creating collages.

3. Their ability to be merged (blended) with other layers using various modes.

4. Their ability to apply selective adjustments using layer masks. In other words, limiting the area to which an adjustment is applied.

5. Layer Styles, which can be used to apply special effects

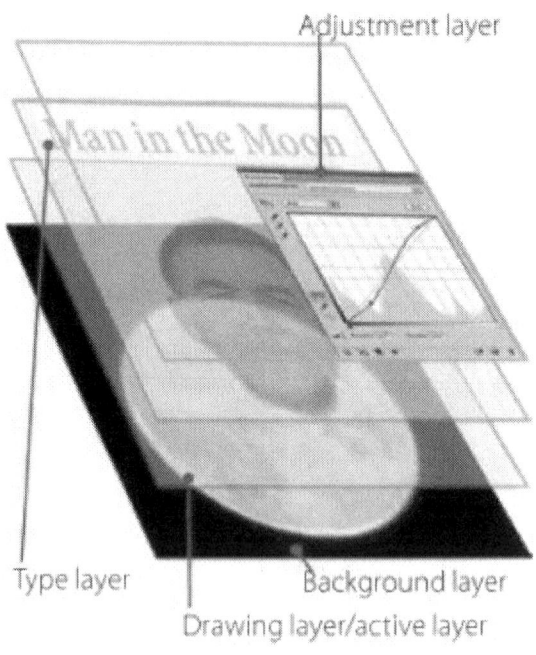

Adjustment layer

Man in the Moon

Type layer

Background layer

Drawing layer/active layer

Layers Filter

Kind of layers are visible

Normal | Opacity: 100%

Lock: | Fill: 100%

Blending mode

Lock: | Fill: 100%

Lock all layer properties

Lock layer position

Lock image pixels

Lock transparent pixels

[1-5] The toolbars in the CS6 Layers panel

Using Layer Style Presets

Layers can be thought of as clear sheets of acetate with images on each sheet. If the sheets of acetate are stacked together, the area where there is no image on a sheet are clear, and allows the image on the layer underneath to show through. Let's take a look at an example.

Open Photoshop Elements, and open a new file with the background filled with white.

You can see the thumbnail image on the background layer in the layers panel shows that it is filled with white. We are going to add some simple graphics to the background layer.

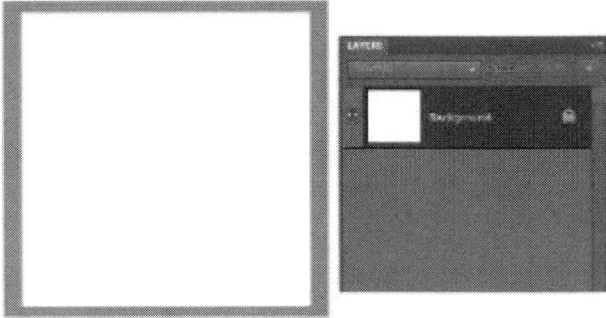

First, use the rectangle marquee tool to draw a rectangle in the background area. Click somewhere in the upper left and while holding down the mouse button, drag down and to the right to create a rectangle. When you let go of the mouse button a dotted line will show up in the window, indicating the selected area. This dotted line is often referred to as the "marching ants".

Next we need to choose a color to fill our selection. Click on the foreground color in the tool panel. When you click on the foreground color the color picker will open. Here you can choose a color by specifying color values in the HSB, RGB, or # boxes (the # box is for hexadecimal values), or you can click on the vertical "rainbow" colored bar in the middle to select a color range, or click in the sample box. As you click, the color chosen will show up in the box under the word "new".

Choose a color you like and click OK. I'm picking a red color. The color chosen becomes the "Foreground Color" in the tools panel. Click on the paint bucket, and click inside the marquee (the marching ants). The rectangle will fill with your foreground color. The thumbnail image in the layers panel will also show the red rectangle. This thumbnail shows everything on that layer.

Once you have the red rectangle, repeat the process using blue and green. You can see in the illustration below that I created three rectangles over the white background; a red rectangle, then a blue rectangle, and a green rectangle on top. You can see the background layer thumbnail in the layer panel.

Here is where the problem is with using just one layer. The background layer is made up of pixels. At first, all the pixels were white. Adding the shapes on the background layer changed the colors of the pixels within our selection from white to red. By creating a selection with the marquee tool and coloring it blue, the white pixels and the red pixels in that selected area were changed to blue. The same thing happened when adding the green rectangle. The white, blue and red pixels in the selected area were changed to green. What if I decide I want the red rectangle to appear on the top of the other rectangles? Since the image is flat, with all the rectangles on one layer, there is no way to select the red rectangle and move it to the top.

I would have to redraw the red rectangle and fill it again to get it on top of the green. Now, that really isn't that big a deal in our example here. Rectangles are pretty easy to draw, but if you are working on your own project, with intricate selections, or multiple photographs, it could cause a lot of problems for you. That's where layers come in.

Creating Layers

Click the "Create a new layer" button (shown in image 1 above). It is located in the bottom left corner of the Layer Panel. A new layer called "Layer 1" is created as shown in image 2 above. The checkerboard pattern in the new layer shows that the layer is transparent; meaning the background layer underneath (the white) will show through it wherever we don't fill Layer 1 with the color.

Click on the new layer "Layer 1" to select it. When a layer is selected it will become darker than the other layers. Add a red rectangle as we did before, using the rectangle marquee tool, the color picker and the paint bucket. Image 3 above shows Layer 1 with the red rectangle. You can still see the transparent part of the layer allowing the white background to show through. Click the "Create a new layer" button again. A new layer called "Layer 2" will be created above the previously selected layer (layer 1). Click on the layer "Layer 2" to select it. That layer in the layer panel will appear dark, indicating it is the layer selected. Create a blue rectangle the same way you did the red rectangle. Do the same to create a green rectangle on a new layer "Layer 3".

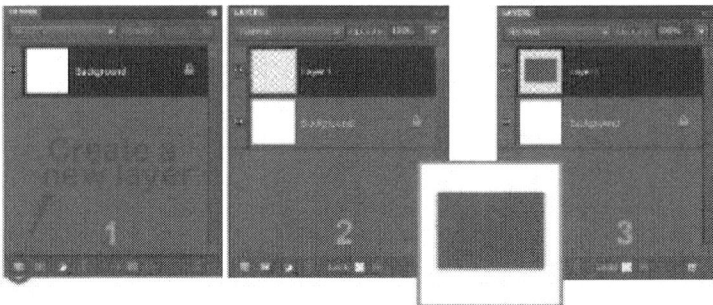

Background Layers

When you first create a Photoshop document, the background layer is automatically created for you. The background layer will always be on the bottom of the layer stack. You will notice there is a padlock in the right side of the layer, indicating that layer is locked. There isn't much you can do with the background layer. Of course you can paint on it as we did before, but there are many things you can't do with it until it becomes a "regular" layer, like all the other layers. There is a way to change it to a regular layer.

Double-click on the background layer. The New Layer dialog box will open where you can name the layer. There are other options you can make in this dialog box. You can accept the default "Layer 0" if you like, or give it a descriptive name. The important thing is, once you click OK, it becomes a regular layer. You can move it up in the stacking order, or do anything to it that you can do to any of the other layers.

Moving Layers

You should now have four layers in the layers panel as shown above, showing the red, blue and green rectangles all on separate layers. Now, if we want to move the blue layer or the red layer to the top, we can do that easily.

Click on the Layer 2 (the layer with the blue rectangle) in the Layers Panel. Click and hold the mouse button down and drag the layer up over Layer 3 (the layer with the green rectangle. When the line above layer 3 becomes bold, let go of the mouse button. Layer 2 will now be above layer 3. You can move layers up and down in the stacking order depending on what images you want to appear "on top" of other images in your artwork. Experiment for yourself. Move the red layer to the top, or move the blue layer under the red layer. You can move any layer, except the background layer, to any position in the stacking order. The background layer always remains at the bottom unless you turn it into a "regular" layer. Let's talk about the background layer for a minute.

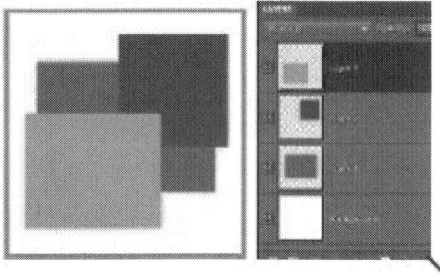

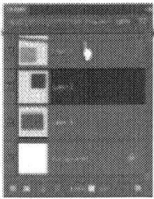

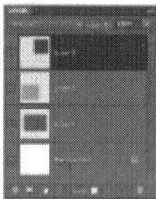

Layer 2 is now on top of Layer 3

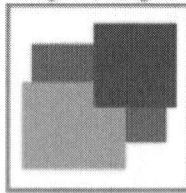

Using Layers to Make Global and Selective Adjustments

Image editing processes generally follow the principle of first the basics, then the details. After you have corrected any major (and some less critical) errors, you can go ahead and fine-tune your results. This has proven time and again to be the most efficient way to approach the image editing process.

But what can we do if an error or an annoying detail becomes apparent only after an image has been processed and enlarged? Or if an image is to be used for a purpose other than the original one? Or if it requires emphasis on elements and colors that previous processing steps didn't account for? Or if we want to adjust various parts of an image using different parameters?

In such cases, it is an enormous help if we can return to corrections we have already made and adjust them.

It is also extremely useful if the corrections we make are performed precisely in easily identifiable steps. If we want corrections, we have already made to remain in place – and this is usually the case – we need to work nondestructively. One of the most established and reliable ways to do this is to work with layers and layer adjustments. Layer functionality is available in many image editors, although Photoshop is still generally recognized as the leader in this field. There are many good reasons to use layer techniques when editing digital images, as you will see.

Chapter 6

Tools in Photoshop

Anatomy of the Toolbox

One of many extremely impressive and additionally the finest, enterprise standard software system on image and also artwork enhancing or development is the Adobe Photoshop, or merely Photoshop. When you're recently preparing in grasping regarding Photoshop, you might probably already know some of its tools plus common editing steps such as resizing and cropping. But, to be able to thoroughly understand as well as master pretty much everything of its tools takes you a huge amount of time. However, you do not need to understand all kinds of things though and thus screw up among Photoshop prime features and extensions even though you still have no idea in relation to it. It's always ideal to make use of Photoshop tutorials to begin with. At this time there a variety of cost-free Photoshop tutorials around the world wide web. Some of them feature

Photoshop tutorials that make use of real world graphic design examples and illustrations.

The primary goal of this document shall be to make you to start with the basic principles of Photoshop (getting started with Photoshop Tools) in order to get started with it. Everyone possess a tendency to skip basic principles or the fundamentals and begin on knowing the advanced and complex Photoshop tutorials in which most people believed is better. But they are completely wrong. Jacob Gube once said, "If you take the time to learn the basics, you'll run into less trouble because you understand how things work."

Let me reveal the full list of Photoshop Tools:

Move Tool (V)

Rectangular Marquee (M)

Elliptical Marquee (M)

Single Row Marquee

Single Column Marquee

Lasso (L)

Polygon Lasso (L)

Magnetic Lasso (L)

Quick Selection (W)

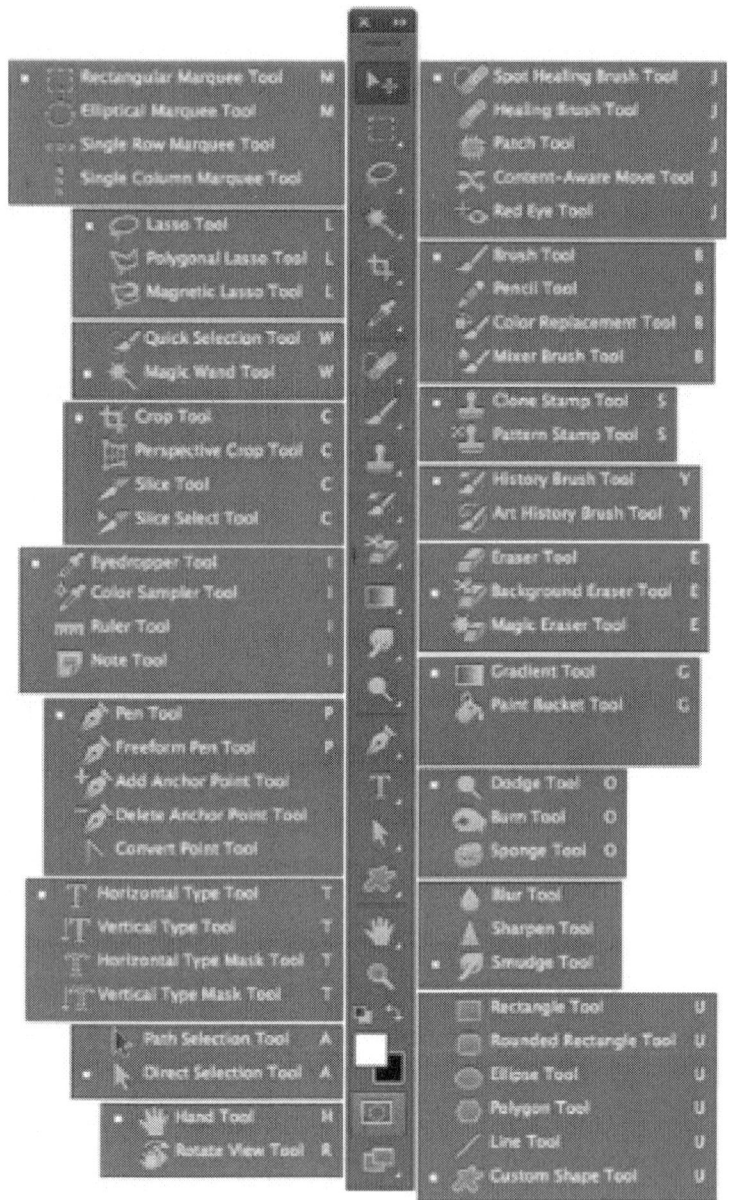

Magic Wand (W)

Crop (C)

Slice (C)

Slice Select (C)

Eyedropper (I)

Color Sampler (I)

Ruler (I)

Note (I)

Spot Healing Brush (J)

Healing Brush (J)

Patch (J)

Red Eye (J)

Brush (B)

Pencil (B)

Color Replacement (J)

Clone Stamp (S)

Pattern Stamp (S)

History Brush (Y)

Art History Brush (Y)

Eraser (E)

Background Eraser (E)

Magic Eraser (E)

Gradient (G)

Paint Bucket (G)

Blur

Sharpen

Smudge

Dodge (O)

Burn (O)

Sponge (O)

Pen (P)

Freeform Pen (P)

Add Anchor Point

Delete Anchor Point

Convert Point

Horizontal Type (T)

Vertical Type (T)

Horizontal Type Mask (T)

Vertical Type Mask (T)

Path Selection (A)

Direct Selection (A)

Rectangle (U)

Rounded Rectangle (U)

Ellipse (U)

Polygon (U)

Line (U)

Custom Shape (U)

Hand (H)

Rotate View (R)

Zoom (Z)

Move Tool

The Move Tool (V) is used to move a selected area or the whole layer. It can be used in conjunction with most of Photoshop's other tools by dragging with the mouse while keeping the Ctrl (Command for Mac) key pressed down.

Move and Copy Shortcut

For the majority of tools, keeping the Ctrl+Alt keys (Command+Option keys for Mac users) pressed as you drag a selection will invoke the Move Tool temporarily, which will let you quickly move the selected layer and duplicate it as well. A whole layer can be duplicated by keeping the Alt key (Option key for Mac users) held down as you use the Move Tool.

Move (Selection Tool, Shortcut V): Use this tool to move the image within the Canvas. Shift-drag constraints 00, 450, 900; opt/alt-drag to duplicate layer.

What you will find in the Options Bar.

Icon: What tool is selected.

Tool Preset: Tool has no default presets.

Auto-Select: When this is selected it allow you to select layers directly in the canvas. Example: You are working on a photo manipulation and during the image arrangement process you can click directly on the image on the canvas and it will activate its layer in the Layers Panel.

Both are saving you time and as well very free flowing in the arrangement of images. You will notice when you activate AutoSelection that other area of the Options Bar will become active.

Layer/Group: Select if you want to work with Layers or Group (if you have created them).

Show Transform Controls: Selecting this will show a Transform

Next to the Transform Controls you will see Icons that are used for lining up objects/images. To have these active you will need to have two or more layers active to make this function. This tool makes lining up objects a breeze.

Selections are one of the most fundamental tasks in Photoshop but it is the first step to so many creative ventures. You can do so many things when you can select and separate parts of your image to provide special treatments or use in other documents. You can duplicate layers, add a new detail or simply add new layers that compliment your existing image. Adding a shadow to your image is a nice touch that adds a bit of life.

We shared the steps for creating an alpha channel so you could separate parts of your image having only those layers appear in your saved file. One you have made selections you can also apply some of Photoshop's special treatment and effects to create new images of your own. What if you wanted to cast a shadow from your building or from someone?

Use the selection tools of your choice. In my case I have a picture of a friend outside of the snow. Using the quick selection tool, I have a nice 'extraction'

showing only my friend in my new image. With this isolated layer, hold the 'Ctrl key' and click on the image portion in the layer thumbnail. When you do this you will select the image you imported. At this point you should see your single 'friend' (or whatever you decided to use) with the selection hyphens showing it completely selected.

With this selected choose from the top menu, 'Select->Transform Selection'. This select command will produce a bounding box around your image. It looks just like the free transform box many are familiar with but it is different. It helps me to compare two similar tools effects when they can be confusing but in this case the same bounding box lets you edit and modify your selection boundary not the selection itself. You could go through these same steps using the free transform tool and when you edit your selection in the next steps, it will actually apply to your selection, in my case a friend's image, not the selection boundary.

With the bounding box in place, choose from the top menu, 'Edit->Transform->Distort' and pull your selection back away from your person in an angle that a shadow would cast. When you do you will see the selection boundary, the moving hyphens drawn down towards the ground. Hit enter to accept your angle and you will see the selection boundary still active.

Now with your selection still active, create a new layer, click on this new layer, and enter a fill for your shadow using the fill option, 'Edit->Fill'. You will see the color fill you chose to fill the selection on a new layer. You have created a shadow for your image.

This is a simple exercise but the fun part is that you can once you have a selection, you can apply effects on a new layer. This lets you separate your selection from your resource image and treat them differently.

In this case we could have turned off our original image and saved a file with only the shadow itself.

You will discover many possibilities with this simple technique of creating selections from existing components, then doing something creative with the selection on new layers.

Inspire, think globally, act locally.

Selection Tools

Selection tools can be used to select particular parts of the document for separate editing i.e. only the area that is selected will be changed as a result of your actions. Selections can be 'feathered' (a fuzzy radius for their edges can be specified) through the Feather field present in the options bar. The example below contains two rectangles – the one on the left was created using a selection with zero pixel 'feathering', and the one on the right was created by using the same selection with a 'feathering' of five pixels.

Marquee tool

Marquee tools (M) can be used to make elliptical or rectangular selections, as well as single column selections (one-pixel wide selection that stretches through the height of the document) and single row selections (a one-pixel-tall selection that stretches through the width of the document). To make single row / single column selections, select the appropriate tool and click on the part of the image where you want to select the row/column.

The Lasso tool

The Lasso tools (L) can be used to make freeform selections. There are three different forms of this tool:

- o Lasso Tool (L): Clicking and dragging this tool will draw a selection area. Release the mouse button to close the selection – the start and end point will be joined automatically by a straight line.

- o Polygonal Lasso Tool (L): Clicking at different points will create the vertices (corners) of a polygon shaped selection. The selection is closed by moving the cursor to the starting vertex and clicking on it once, or by hitting Enter.

- o Magnetic Lasso Tool (L): If the selection you want to make is complex, you can use the

Magnetic Lasso Tool for help. Photoshop will try to make an intelligent selection by following edges of color difference and contrast (the difference between light and dark). With the Magnetic Lasso Tool (L) selected, click a single time near the 'edge' of the object you wish to select and follow around its edges – a selection path will automatically be created in Photoshop. While you're following the edges, click on a point to force a selection point to be created on the selection path.

The selection is closed by hitting Enter or by clicking at the point where you started. Once a selection has been made, only the pixels inside are active and modifiable. Many tools can be used without having to make a selection. But you should also know that if you haven't made specifically selected a part of the layer, Photoshop will assume that you're working with the whole layer and the changes you make will affect all of the pixels inside this layer.

A comprehensive example

Typically, when we begin making selections we want to modify our existing image, 'clean it up' a bit, or provide a different backdrop. A new world of possibility opens up when we begin using the selections themselves for new material and creative ways to expand on our source image.

The first step and lesson begin the understanding that once you make a selection, you can address it and 'dress it' on another layer. This is a lot. You might want to duplicate an image. You might want to duplicate an image but show some inverse contrast to its colors. You can even create patterns on others layers beginning with the source image and the selection you choose.

What if you have two images you want to blend by having part of the backdrop show through the 'top' image? I have a lovely rainbow and a glowing full moon. I want the moon in the backdrop to show through the top image blending with it. It is easy to create selections and move them, move the content inside the selection. The most important reminders are paying attention to what layer you have selected, and also the little icon indicating what mode your selection is in.

In my case, I am going to create a selection that will allow the moon to shine through. To be sure I choose the right area, I will first turn off the visibility of the top layer, my rainbow. Now I will create a selection of my moonbeam. When I make this selection, I see the selection icon showing the little dots indicating my selection mode. In this mode I can move the selection boundary fine tuning on what will be selected. However, with this selection active, if I choose the move tool from the toolbar and hover back over my selection, I see instead little scissors indicating I will move the selection contents, not the boundary.

This is a good exercise because little details like this and the messages Photoshop is providing, in this case the selection mode, make all the difference in a quick simple modification versus wondering why it's not working at all. You can move your selection boundary with your keyboard arrows too.

Once you feel like you have the portion you want to show through, turn your top layer back on and choose this top layer with your mouse. Now choose the move tool and move the contents away! You have created a little window allowing the backdrop, the image behind, to show through blending their images together.

You can have a lot of fun with this exercise. You could even import into After Effects and animate this view opening up. Remember that to 'unselect' your selection simply enter 'Ctrl D' from the keyboard and to 'move backwards' on the steps you've committed, enter 'Alt-Ctrl-Z' or choose the editing direction options from the Edit command in the top toolbar.

Crop Tool

The Crop Tool (C) is used for trimming images.

Make a selection using the Crop Tool and double click at the selection's center, or hit Enter, to crop the image to the selection (i.e. the part of the image which is outside the selection will be deleted).

To cancel the crop selection without cropping, hit the Esc key or select another tool.

Cropping outside the box

The Crop tool can be used for resizing your canvas. Expand the document window until it is larger than the area of your image, and now make a crop selection which includes all of your image as well as some of the gray area outside your image. If you apply this crop selection, you canvas will include the image as well as the extra area you selected (the canvas gets extended).

The Magic Want Tool (W)

The Magic Want Tool (W) will select parts of the image that have a similar color. The tolerance of the Magic Wand selection can be varied; think of the tolerance as the required closeness of the color values, to the color of the region you have clicked on, in order for them to be added to the selection.

You can also choose whether you want a contiguous selection (pixels are touching) or not (colors that fall within the specified tolerance range will be selected throughout the document, even if the regions aren't touching each other).

Selection Tasks and Shortcuts

Hold down the Shift key to add another region to an existing selection. Keep the Alt key (Option key for Mac users) held down to select the intersection (region common to two selections) of your first and second selections. The arrow keys on your keyboard can be used to move the selection one pixel at a time. If this isn't fast enough for you, use the arrow keys with the Shift key held down to move the selection at a rate of ten pixels.

The Ctrl+J (Command+J for Mac) keyboard shortcut can be used to copy your selection to its original layer. In order to cut the selection from its own layer, use Shift+Ctrl+J (or Shift+Comand+J) for Mac. In order to deselect a selected area, click outside of the area while having one of the Marquee tools selected, or use the Ctrl+D (Command+D for Mac) keyboard shortcut. In order to reactivate you most recent selection, use Shift+Ctrl+D (Shift+Command+D for Mac) keyboard shortcut.

The Text Tool

The Text Tool (T), as its name implies, is used for creating text layers. It is quite easy to use, simply select the tool, click on the area you want the text to go and begin to type it in. By clicking and dragging with the Text tool you can make a rectangular area which will force the text to wrap around its boundaries. The color, font size and other settings can be changed from the options bar.

With the Text tool active, you're able to move your cursor out of the text area. The cursor symbol will change from the 'text insert' symbol to the 'move' symbol, indicating that you can now move your text layer around.

Also keep in mind that when this tool is active, you aren't able to use keyboard shortcuts for accessing other tools. It may seem quite obvious right now, but it can easily escape your mind when you're concentrated on your image and strange characters start appearing in your active text box because you were attempting to use keyboard shortcuts.

When you're done typing, hit Ctrl+Enter (Command+Return for Mac users), after which you will be able to use your keyboard shortcuts as before.

Shape Tools

You can make shapes by click-dragging the Rectangle, Rounded Rectangle, Ellipse, Polygon, Line and Custom Shape tools (U).

The particular settings for each of these shape tools are present in the options bar, and you can specify other settings by clicking on the arrow to the Custom Shape button's right side. For instance, the Line Tool can be set to display arrowheads, and you can also specify the sizes and shapes of these arrowheads, as illustrated below:

If you observe the options for these shapes, you'll see that there are three methods for making a shape:

Your shape will be made as a single colored layer which is covered with a vector shape mask.

Confusing right? Imagine the vector mask to be a sheet of dark paper with a hole (in the shape you have drawn) cut through it so that you're able to see the color which comes out of the hole. To change the color of your shape, select the Shape tool, and in the options bar, pick a color from the Fill menu. Make sure that you have selected 'Shape' from the

Shape/Path/Pixels drop down box, also present in the options bar.

When you selected 'Path' in the Shape/Path/Pixels menu, the shape is created as a path, which you can see in the Paths palette (see the example above, where this shape is called the Work Path).

When you choose 'Pixels', the shape is 'drawn' on whichever layer you have presently selected. In the example, this shape was drawn on the Layer 0 layer, as you can see from the Layers palette.

Color Selection

You can set foreground and background colors by clicking on their color tiles and picking a color using the Color Picker, which you can see demonstrated below:

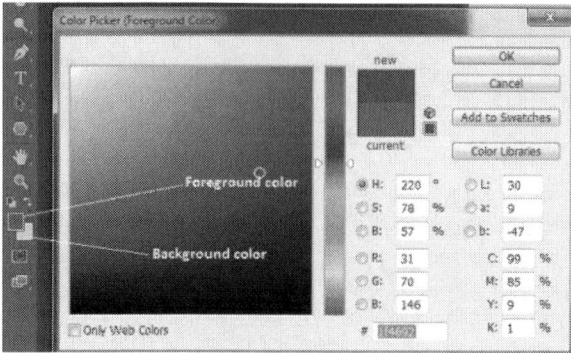

Shortcuts for the Color

Picker

You can press X on the keyboard to switch between foreground and background colors. Hit the D key to revert to the default black/white foreground/background combination.

You can also use the Eyedropper Tool to sample another color from your picture and make this the foreground color. All you need to do is click inside the document window, move your cursor to the color you want to select and click on it.

You can also set the background color using this tool. Select colors using the eyedropper tool with the Alt key (Option key for Mac users) pressed down, to do so.

The Paint Bucket, Paint Brush, Pencil as well as all other drawing/painting tools can be changed temporarily to the Eyedropper Tool by pressing down the Alt (Option) key.

Painting Tools

Besides Photoshop's amazing photo editing capabilities, it also has painting and drawing tools which let you create your own backgrounds and shapes.

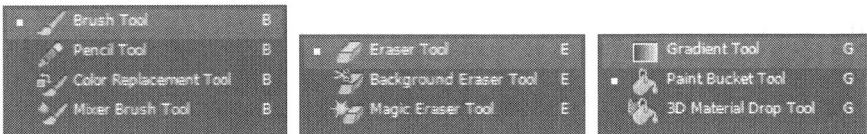

The Brush Tool

The Brush Tool (B) is suited for soft-edged drawing or painting. You can draw strokes by clicking and dragging your mouse cursor over the canvas. The brush size, as well as other settings, can be changed from the options bar.

The Pencil Tool

The Pencil Tool (B) is meant for hard-edged painting or drawing and has options similar to the Brush tool for specifying its opacity, size etc. This tool is commonly used for editing individual pixels in zoomed images.

The Eraser Tool

The Eraser Tool (E) erases pixels from your canvas. You can choose Block, Pencil or Brush modes from the Mode menu present in the options bar. Aliased or anti-aliased? The edges of the Pencil Tool's drawing are aliased as opposed to anti-aliased edges of the Brush Tool. 'Aliasing' refers to the jags that appear on the edges of an object, whereas anti-aliasing refers to the absence (or removal) of these jags i.e. the edges are smooth. In the example present below, the difference in terms of jagging of the edges between the two sets of shapes is quite visible.

The Paint Bucket Tool

The Paint Bucket Tool (G) will fill a selection with a plain color, also called a flat color. To use it, click on the area you wish to fill once. If this area isn't part of selection, the tool will fill all similar colored pixels within the region of the click.

The Gradient Tool

The Gradient Tool (G) will fill a selection with a mix of multiple colors called a gradient. It is easy to make your own gradient, or you could use the preset gradients present in Photoshop.

Click on the small triangle to the right of the currently selected Gradient pattern in the Options bar to reveal the preset gradients

Apply the gradient by setting your required foreground and background colors, choosing a pattern, then click-dragging your cursor over the area you want to be filled. You already know what the background is, think of the foreground as the front portions of the image i.e. the ones which seem closer in the picture when you look at it.

In my experience, the foreground to background and foreground to transparent gradients are the most commonly used (the first two gradients in the drop down menu). The first will mix the foreground color with the background color, whereas the second will mix the foreground color into a transparent background, yielding a 'fading out' look.

The Hand Tool

You can move your canvas around using the Hand Tool (H) which is useful when you've zoomed in an image or have opened a very large image.

Conveniently, you can also use this tool while you have any other tool selected (excluding the Text Tool) by keeping the spacebar pressed. This is great for positioning your image just where you desire without having to switch between tools.

Other Useful Shortcuts and Tasks

- Zooming: If you want to make a tiny change at the pixel level, you will have to zoom right into your image. Press Ctrl and + together for zooming in, and Ctrl and - for zooming out. You can also specify a zoom value in the text box present at the right side of the status bar

- Creating a Selection Using the Layers Palette: If you want to select all the pixels of a specific layer, click a layer's thumbnail (present in the Layer's palette) while keeping the Ctrl key (Command key for Mac users) pressed down. The transparency level of the layers pixels will also be taken into account with this selection, so if you paint inside the selection, Photoshop will imitate the original layer's transparency settings. The example below shows how I selected the pixels in a text layer using this method:

- Selecting through a Quick Mask: Quick Masks are one of graphic designing's trade secrets which are frequently employed by professionals, but are quite intimidating for beginners. The truth is, they aren't as complicated as they appear:

Quick Mask

Think of a Quick Mask as a different way of creating a selection. Start by entering the Quick Mask Mode (Q) and paint over the things you don't want to select by using tools such as the Brush Tool. You are now painting the 'mask', and the reverse-selection which results will show as a semitransparent red color, as in the example below:

The painting and drawing tools can be used to edit this layer as you want, without affecting your actual image. The changes you make will reflect in your final selection, which is made when you switch back to Standard Mode (Q).

There are two advantages of using this method of selection instead of the normal selection tools that you were taught previously:

- They let you control the transparency level of the selection.

- Coloring an object into select it is easier than having to make a line around it.

At first, it might be hard to grasp that you aren't in fact painting your actual image while you are in the Quick Make Mode; you are simply painting your selection. Once you understand this however, you will be comfortable with making a selection regardless of the shape of the object, no matter how tricky it appears to be.

Quick Mask Options

If you want the see through red of the Quick Mask Mode to show the selected areas instead of the excluded areas, you can do so through the Quick Mask Options. Double-click the Quick Mask Mode icon and change the setting present under the Color Indicates section to 'Selected Areas':

Chapter 7

Elements in Photoshop

Whenever you do not want to mess especially when it comes to the actual specifics, or perhaps when you're conscious a image wants only a little bit of fine-tuning but you need more control of things within the alterations, you just need to use the option of Quick Fix that come with Photoshop Elements as you will soon find out in this brand new selection of tutorials.

Photoshop Elements being an image manager, permits anyone to make modifications that would be completely impossible in years past. But nowadays you do not just need to be a graphic expert, since the computer will do the actual work for you, examining photos as well as correcting them instantly with the Photoshop Elements quick fix functions.

So in order to edit photos in Quick Fix, we need to:

1) Open up a file within Photoshop Elements after which select Edit Quick in the Edit pane's drop down menu, so that the Quick Fix workspace opens

2) Tips on how to set view options:- Through the view menus positioned beneath the image, choose whether or not you want to see the actual end result (After Only), the first (Before Only), or an evaluation layout (together the Before as well as After options)

3) Make use of the Zoom field and slider to specify just how zoomed-in you would like it to end up being. In the Before and After displays, the zoom degree relates to the two versions. When the Zoom or even Hand tool is active, you can also click on the actual pixels, Fit Screen, or Printing Size control keys to switch to those zoom ranges.

4) It in no way hurts to play around with the Smart Fix slider. Smart Fix sets lighting, color, and also sharpening according to its calculations. In some cases, this may be the sole edit you need.

As soon as you have finished editing the picture, be sure you save it as being a new data file, just in case you decide that you would like to change the first picture once more.

Chapter 8

Important Maneuvers

The Window menu is also useful. It has a list consisting of the fourth element of the Basic Photoshop interface, namely panels or palettes. More about these soon. The Help menu can also be of use. Hit F1 to go online to Adobe.com or various forums about Photoshop. If you find yourself getting stuck or being unable to remember how to use a feature of the program, just use the Help to find an answer to your question. The small text field near the top right corner of the screen is also useful. Just type a topic into the field and hit Enter to be taken to the online Help.

The panels or palettes on the right side of the screen are the fourth element of the Photoshop CS6 interface. To expand the palettes, just click the two-headed arrow. To show a palette, click a tab one time. Double-clicking a tab will let you open or close a palette. Clicking the divider between two panels and dragging it will let you resize them. These palettes work with each of the tools, and we will do more with them in subsequent blog posts about Photoshop Basics.

At this time, take a look at the small options buttons located on the top right corner of a palette. This lists all of the options that are available for that particular palette. You can also find the main options on the palette's bottom row.

If you want to customize the interface in Photoshop, click on a palette tab and drag it to the center of the screen. Palettes can also be closed by clicking the small "x" in the top right corner. They can also be stacked in different ways, though doing so makes it easy to lose track of your palettes. If you need to find a lost palette, use the Window menu and click on the one you are looking for. It is hard to actually lose something in Photoshop.

If you need to reset your workspace back to the default settings, go to the Window menu, select Workspace, and then Default Workspace. This option is also available in the Workspace Shifter dropdown list in the top right corner. You can also save any favorite configurations for later use.

One of the most useful menus in Photoshop today is the Window drop down menu. In this menu you'll see a list consisting of the fourth element of Basic interface. These panels or palettes, as some refer to them, work together with the tools in the program. The Help menu is also a very useful menu that you'll find in the upper right corner or, using the F1 Help takes you directly online to the Adobe.com and other Photoshop forums. When you're stuck or want to recall how to do a specific task, you can jump directly to the help system and easily locate the answer to your question. You can also type your search word into the text box and easily find the topic that way. This is a very user friendly program.

Another element of the Photoshop interface is the panels (or palettes). These are located on the right hand of your screen. You simply click on the double arrow which expands the palettes. Now you can click on the tab showing the palette and select your choice. If you wish to make them larger, simply click and drag them with the dividing line. They readily work together with the tools and will help you in making your photo look as you desire. Using the small flyout choice on the top right will give you a list of the options that are available on any specific palette. These options are also on the bottom row of the palette.

If you wish to customize your interface for Photoshop, you can simply click and drag any palette tab to the middle of your screen. Close palettes through clicking the small cross on the right or you can stack them into a different configuration to make things more convenient for your specific needs. Don't worry; you can't lose anything while doing this in Adobe. You can easily reset the workspace as well using the top right workspace shifter drop down list. Be sure to save your favorite configuration.

Lastly, you'll want to look on the lower left of the image. Here a small box with available file sizes resides. The first size you'll see is for the layers flattened, and then you'll see the layers intact. We'll go into this discussion more in a future blog post.

Now that you know what you're doing, it's easy to see that nothing has really changed a whole lot in the recent versions. Sometimes Adobe adds in a new tool or function on the menus, but these are usually self-explanatory and easy to navigate. Basically, there is no real difference between working in Photoshop on your PC and on a Mac. Computer.

Chapter 9

Easy tips:

Photoshop is one of the best graphic tools available for designers and photographers. There is a lot you can do and make with Photoshop. However, before reaching the advanced tools and techniques, it is important to master the basics of this platform.

If you are just starting out with this image editing software, here are some tips you can put to use:

1.) Customized Workspace- To create a project-specific workspace, simply choose and arrange the components and palettes per your needs. Then select: Windows>Workspace>Save Workspace.

You can choose a specific name for your workspace and save it, so it is available for future use. Creating customized workspaces can improve your productivity and help save time.

2.) Displaying Image in Two Windows- When you are working with an image, you might need to take a zoomed in view or a closer look at the picture to make any changes. To make sure that the changes look fine on the normal image, you can open a single image in two windows - one that will display the Normal View and one with the 'Zoom in' view, where you will make the changes. This saves time as you will not need to zoom in and zoom out again and again to check how the image looks.

3.) Using the Undo Feature- While making changes to an image, you can easily undo the changes by simply pressing CTRL+Z (windows shortcut for undo). This is a great shortcut you can use during first Photoshop training, as you will need to keep toggling back and forth to see the effects of your changes.

4.) Changing Background and Foreground Colors- An interesting feature of Photoshop is that it allows you switch foreground and background colors for an image. Clicking on the color square will open the complete color panel, so you can choose the colors of your choice. To switch colors, simply press X. To restore the default color setting i.e. black as the foreground and white as the background color, simply press D.

5.) Opening Documents- To open a document, you do not need to reach out for the File Menu every time and then open a new document from there. You can simply double-click on the Grey window background on the Photoshop page, and a new document will open up.

6.) Viewing Individual Files- When you open multiple files, Photoshop cascades them which can make it difficult for you to view each file. To deal with this, you can perform a simple step:

Select Windows>Arrange>Tile. This results in re-arrangement of all the open files in a way that they are all visible at once. You can also close them all at once by using CTRL+W (Shortcut for Close All).

Conclusion

Starting off from the Beginning

The primary things to watch out for in picking some sort of short training program over the Internet is to be sure that the short training addresses first the essential rather than jumping in immediately towards the complicated things. That is really helpful, specifically in case you are really new to working with Adobe Elements altogether. By giving you an introduction to where to find each one of the different fundamental tools found in the majority of projects, it will be much easier for you to think about much more sophisticated methods and in the end turn out to be more and more self-confident to experiment on the various elements that may be carried out by using this software package.

Video lessons

Another thing to look for in any tutorial course on the Internet is actually whether or not you can find educational videos that could guide you through certain basic techniques and procedures. Often, Adobe Photoshop Elements tutorials that are discovered online are created by people who have a very good know-how on the use of the computer software. What could seem to them as sheer basic directions could sound very vague as well as confusing for any man or women very new to the particular computer software! With the video guide, it is possible to comprehend what they are talking about and follow these step-by-step, temporarily halting the video every now and then in order to make certain you are doing it effectively.

Programs

Last but not least, be sure that the tutorial program that you will be using will take care of those applications as well as techniques that you will need the most. There are a number of course websites online that enlist the actual guide pages through sections. They're great because you could maximize your time in merely learning things you need. Nothing could be very more annoying on the part of the individual wanting to learn the ins and outs of Adobe Photoshop Elements by wasting too much effort finding out elements which might be self-explanatory and could be not able to go to progress except if this chapter is accomplished.

Thank you for taking time in reading this book. I believe it has been informative in learning Photoshop and giving you a baseline of what Photoshop really is.

Thank you again for downloading this book!

Finally, if you enjoyed this book, then I'd like to ask you for a favor, would you be kind enough to leave a review for this book on Amazon? It'd be greatly appreciated!

Thank you and good luck!

Bonus: preview of: Google Drive: A Beginner's Guide to Google Drive: Master Google Drive, Docs, Sheets, and Slides Now

This book contains proven steps and strategies on how to use Google Drive to the fullest.

This eBook will explain the basics of Google Drive and how people can benefit from it. By reading this book, you will know how to create, upload, edit, share, remove, and restore files using the Google Drive system. In addition, you will learn how to use Docs, Sheets, and Slides – powerful services from Google that you can use for free.

Click here to check out the rest on Amazon.

Made in the USA
Charleston, SC
03 August 2016